HOW TO WRITE
SIMPLE AND EFFECTIVE
LETTERS OF
INTENT
IN JUST
500
WORDS

To my twin sister Emma, my dad, Tommy Westwood and my mum, Maralyn Westwood, who taught me the importance of simplicity, wordplay and talking respectively, while also instilling the value of trust that has become central to my work and is essential in contracts.

HOW TO WRITE
SIMPLE AND EFFECTIVE
LETTERS OF
INTENT
IN JUST
500
WORDS

SARAH FOX

500
W O R D S

Copyright © 2016 – Sarah Jane Victoria Fox

First published in Great Britain in 2016

Published by
500 Words Ltd
Ash Cottage
Hawthorn Lane
Wilmslow
Cheshire
SK9 5DG

A catalogue record for this book is available from the British Library.

ISBN: 978-0-9955409-0-3

Book design and typesetting by Ashdown Creative
www.ashdowncreative.co.uk

Cover photograph © Fotolia.com

CONTENTS

PREFACE

This book by Sarah Fox is about 'Letters of Intent'. Truth to tell, it is all about how to write in simple everyday and practical language, about those beloved Letters of Intent. The acronym 'KISS' is apt. Sarah *"Keeps it simple stupid"*. Even better is the label "Keep it short & simple". She is ever so keen to get you to keep to her 500-words theme. Her firm is even called '500 Words Ltd'. I like that idea. There is more. Her theme also brings in those 'Six honest serving-men', courtesy of Rudyard Kipling: *"I keep six honest serving-men,(they taught me all I know): their names are What and Why and When and How and Where and Who."* Her 98 pages are devoted to doing the opposite to what an awful lot of other lawyers tell you not to do ... Sarah actually wants you to use Letters of Intent; others say don't. Mind you, she insists that you craft the LOI to her design and have it down to, yes, 500 words.

The real bug in Letters of Intent over all these years has been industry not drilling down to properly understand what they are but also why they are needed at all. So her 98-page book tells you what these mini contracts are and how to make them work well and what's to be done to properly adopt this very important topic. I confess that once I had read Sarah's practical guide (that's what it is), I began to shed my shivers, warming to this hitherto famous area for disputes. Indeed another theme in the book is avoiding disputes about Letters of Intent.

Sarah teases out: Why you should write simple LOI, note simple, then how you (yes you) can write certain Letters of Intent. Then writing effective LOI. By now you will recognise in the book her four critical contents and what she calls her six effective extras. She underpins that systematic approach with her theme and demand for simple, robust and workable Letters of Intent.

Yes I know that construction industry contracts of 50,000 words dominate our landscape and so too no end of amendments. Sarah at 500 Words *"sends them abroad on her own affairs, from the second she opens her eyes … one million Hows, two million Wheres and seven million Whys!"*

Tony Bingham
Barrister, arbitrator and columnist

3 Paper Buildings
Temple
LONDON
EC4Y 7EU

INTRODUCTION

The UK construction industry is plagued by letters of intent that are disasters waiting to happen. Their vague content means that the client cannot be sure what the contractor is meant to do and when the contractor is meant to stop.

Rather than telling you to avoid letters of intent, this book takes a different approach: it will act as your guide to writing a letter of intent that is crystal clear, keeps your project on schedule, and will never rumble on. In just a few pages, you will learn the critical content your letter of intent needs and how to use it effectively as a temporary fix. You will be sure what works the contractor can and cannot do, precisely when it should have completed those works, and how much it will be paid.

Why Letters of Intent?

Letters of intent, like all legal agreements, are tools to *help you do business*. Like any tool in your business tool box, a letter of intent should be fit for its intended purpose, and used in the right way.

Most existing letters of intent are not fit for purpose. For example, although the purpose of all letters of intent is to make sure your project finishes on time, no examples I have seen *oblige* the contractor to complete the initial works by a precise date.

Most letters of intent are not used in the right way. For example, in 2014 an English court said that a project manager was *negligent* when he allowed a project to continue under a letter of intent, without explaining the risks to his client. This book will show you how to use your letter of intent effectively as a temporary fix.

During my 15 years as a construction solicitor with Eversheds LLP, and now as an independent consultant, I reviewed hundreds of examples of and cases on letters of intent. This book shares what I've learnt to help you to write better letters and use them successfully.

Why 500 Words?

Unlike the vague versions, a 500-word letter of intent positively encourages you to get the full contract signed. You and your contractor will read and understand it, and you won't mistake it for the fully-functioning contract for the whole project. You will realise it is just the first step in the contract negotiation process, not the last step.

In 2012, my twin sister challenged me to write a letter of intent in just 500 words: that's a single A4 page. I started from scratch and created a letter that is simple, uncluttered, easy to use, and legally robust. Although shorter than all the ones my clients have seen before, it contains more relevant content. This book explains how you can do it too. It also convinces you to change by explaining why a 500-word letter of intent is a good idea (at least until you enter into the full contract).

Who Should Read This Book?

This book is written for:

- Contracts managers, lawyers, your company 'contracts expert' and consultants who write or review letters of intent

- Banks and investors who want to know if the financial limits in the letter of intent are effective

- Consultants advising employers who want to understand and explain the pitfalls of using letters of intent to avoid being negligent

- Contract administrators who want to know how to operate the procedures in the letter of intent properly

- Contractors who want to know whether they will get paid.

One Friday afternoon, you may be told that the project absolutely *has* to start on Monday and it's up to you to sort out the paperwork and get it signed on the dotted line. What should you do? You need to make sure your letter of intent is effective and a good one – one *you can read, understand and use.*

The Structure

After explaining what a letter of intent is, this book is presented in 4 parts:

Part A: Why you should write simple letters of intent. Long letters of intent are the norm in the UK construction industry, so this Part highlights the benefits of shorter, more readable, more usable letters of intent. It explains the five legal requirements you need for your letter of intent to be legally binding, and why you should use a simple letter of intent.

Part B: How you can write certain letters of intent. This sets out the four critical contents your letter of intent needs to be legally binding. It takes you step-by-step through how to avoid common errors, what happens if you add nothing to your letter, then why and how you can write it simply.

Part C: How you can write effective letters of intent. This introduces six effective extras which help you to create a workable letter of intent. It takes the same step-by-step approach as Part B, and concludes with reminding you of some clauses you don't need.

Part D: Next steps for letter of intent success. This summarises how to use your letter of intent successfully. It helps you to ask better questions before you send it and provides a 10-Point Scorecard to review its contents.

I have written the chapters in 500-word blocks, to demonstrate that even complex legal issues do not require long-winded explanations. As that is true of legal issues, you will realise how much easier it can be to describe construction works in just 500 words.

How To Read This Book

The book is short, so it won't take you long to read. You should read it from start to finish, and mark sections which you know you'll want to return to before you start your next project. By applying its tips, you will create a letter of intent that is simple, easy to use, and legally robust.

This book reflects the laws of England/Wales. As a user guide, this book is not a comprehensive explanation of all the relevant cases or statutes, nor is it a substitute for legal advice. Depending on your previous experience, you may want to check whether it is the right time to use a letter of intent, or get your lawyer to review that your content is a good fit for your contractor and your valuable project.

1

WHAT IS A LETTER OF INTENT?

A letter of intent is just a specialised short form of contract, in the style of a letter. It is widely used in the UK construction industry to get a project started with the minimum of paperwork.

The term 'letter of intent' covers everything from a 1-page letter confirming the company with whom you want to contract, through a wide spectrum to a 17-page fully-functional contract. At its core is a letter that says:

- the *Client* (the sender)[1] intends to enter into a full contract with the Contractor for a project – the *intention* element of the letter of intent

- the *Contractor* (the recipient) is asked or instructed to start some preparatory works, order specific long-lead materials and goods, or provide some pre-contract services.

A Letter of Intent is Legally Binding

It is part of the folklore of the construction industry that there exists a mythical beast, 'the Letter of Intent', the legal effect of which, if it is acted upon, is that it entitles a contractor to payment … but does not expose him to any risk because it imposes no contractual obligations on him.[2]

Historically, letters of intent were not contracts. They were documents that provided comfort to a contractor that it would be appointed on the project, but they were not binding on the parties. A non-binding letter of intent might have worked in the *good old days* but, in our increasingly sophisticated world, a modern letter of intent needs to create legally binding obligations for both the Client and Contractor.

Any letter of intent that is deliberately written to be non-binding means the Contractor provides works, goods and services 'at risk'; i.e. at risk of not being paid. This strategy is rarely adopted in the UK construction industry. A letter of intent can be *accidentally* non-binding if it fails to meet any one of the five legal requirements for a contract (Part B), or is marked 'subject to contract' (Chapter 22).

A Letter of Intent Helps You Do Business

As with other legally binding agreements, the purpose of a letter of intent is to *help you to do business*. A letter of intent should help you to do business by starting your project quickly *and* keeping your project to time. In the UK, most examples meet the first purpose but very few meet the latter.

As a tool to help you do business, your letter of intent should clearly record what each party has agreed. This prevents misunderstandings, and means the letter acts as a guide to what you (and your Contractor) need to do. This type of letter of intent will also help you avoid disputes.

A Letter of Intent is a Construction Contract

A letter of intent is a 'construction contract'[3] as defined by UK legislation; i.e. an agreement recording the details of works, installation of materials, or services to be provided for a building, development, or construction project. As a construction contract, it needs to meet certain minimum requirements on payment (Chapter 12).

2

WHAT A LETTER OF INTENT IS NOT

A letter of intent is not:

A LETTER OF COMFORT

This is a letter sent by a Client to a Contractor which says the Client intends to enter into the full contract sometime in the future. It neither instructs nor authorises the Contractor to start works, order materials and goods, or provide services. Your letter of intent could mistakenly be a letter of comfort if it fails to authorise, or actually prohibits the Contractor from carrying out, any works.

> **TIP:** To create a letter of intent, ensure your letter asks or instructs the Contractor to provide works, goods, or services (Chapter 11).

A LETTER OF ACCEPTANCE

This is a letter sent by a Client to a Contractor which says the Client accepts the Contractor's tender. As the Contractor's tender is an offer to carry out the project, a letter of acceptance can accept that tender and create a contract for the whole project (Chapter 4).

> **TIP:** To create a letter of intent for limited works, avoid all reference to the Contractor's tender (Chapter 20).

HEADS OF TERMS

This is a document sent by (or on behalf of) a Client to a Contractor which identifies key terms such as the parties, works, price, time, as well as the standard form on which the full contract will be based. It is used to summarise correspondence, documents and meetings, as the basis for further discussions. Your letter of intent is in danger of becoming a heads of terms document if you misguidedly include an overview of the current state of negotiations.

> **TIP:** To create a letter of intent, avoid including any details relevant only to the full contract.

THE FULL CONTRACT

This is the comprehensive contract covering the four critical contents, six effective extras, as well as a detailed explanation of how the works will be carried out and administered. Commonly it will be over 50 pages and 25,000 words and cover every eventuality for the project. Your letter of intent, on the other hand, is to be a temporary contract for limited works and is not designed for the whole project.

> **TIP:** To ensure your letter of intent is not the *only* contract, include a right to terminate it (Chapter 6) and focus on getting the full contact signed (Chapter 23).

AN INCENTIVE TO SIGN THE FULL CONTRACT

A letter of intent is rarely effective at persuading the Contractor to sign on the dotted line. Once the initial works start, the parties will take their eye off the ball and just get down to work. Negotiating the terms of the full contract will be the last thing on the parties' to-do lists. As the Contactor is often paid for *any* works it carries out (not just the ones mentioned in your letter), it has no real incentive to sign the full contract.

> **TIP:** Focus on practical steps to get the full contract signed (Part D), rather than assuming the terms of your letter act as an incentive.

3

TEN FREQUENTLY ASKED QUESTIONS

1 **Is it ever OK to use a letter of intent?** It is not negligent to start a project under a letter of intent. However, you could be negligent in letting a project *continue* under a letter of intent, especially if you don't understand the pitfalls (Part D).

2 **What's wrong with letters of intent?** Letters of intent often have plenty of content, but not the right sort. Part B will introduce the four critical contents your letter of intent needs and Part C six extras to make your letter of intent effective.

3 **Can you avoid letters of intent?** You could just say *No* and refuse to use one – but that will not start your project quickly. Or you could use a short form standard contract to cover the initial works – but that might delay the start. Parts B and C will show you how to quickly create a 500-word letter of intent to start your project now and protect the parties.

4 **Why do disputes happen?** A major cause of disputes is that the parties misunderstand the impact of a letter of intent. You may think the letter is a merely a tool to start the project quickly and is otherwise risk-free. Meanwhile, the Contractor thinks the letter of intent is a blank cheque and it can carry out the whole project. You need to realise that your letter of intent is the *first stage* in your contract negotiation process, not its end.

5 **What can be done to minimise the risk of disputes?** To help you avoid disputes you should write simple letters of intent (Parts B and C) to avoid the above misunderstandings. You should also learn how to use letters of intent correctly (Part D).

6 **What's the main risk in *writing* a letter of intent?** If you don't ask *why* you are using a letter of intent, your letter won't help you achieve that purpose, as it won't cover the right issues (Chapter 9).

7 **What's the main risk in *using* a letter of intent?** The main risk is that a full contract is never signed and the works rumble on (Chapter 15 and Part D).

8 **What happens if the full contract is not entered into?** Unless the letter of intent is terminated, the Contractor may continue to carry out works, but no-one knows what terms apply and you end up in a contractual no-man's land (Chapter 23).

9 **How can you encourage the Contractor to enter into the full contract?** First, you need to create a letter of intent for very limited initial works (Chapters 6 and 11). Second, you need to focus your efforts on getting your Contractor to agree the full contract (Part D).

10 **Why can't you rely on the limits in your letter of intent?** In the majority of cases, where a letter of intent contains limits on price, works or time and the Contractor exceeds those limits, it still gets paid (Chapter 20).

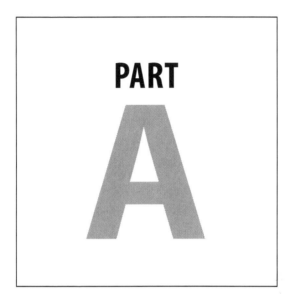

PART

WHY YOU SHOULD WRITE SIMPLE LETTERS OF INTENT

This Part explores what you need for a contract and considers three key reasons to write simple letters of intent:

1 **To get your project started.** The whole purpose of using a letter of intent is to create an agreement to allow the project to get started *now*. Chapter 5 explains how your simple letter of intent will help you start your project quicker, as the letter can be agreed quickly.

2 **To record your agreement.** One-third of UK construction projects[4] start without *any* form of contract. If you want to start your project with a contract, you need to write a letter of intent that is a temporary contract for limited works. Chapter 6 explains how.

3 **To avoid disputes.** The main causes of worldwide construction disputes arise from failures to *read*, *understand* and effectively *use* contracts. If you want to avoid disputes, then Chapter 7 demonstrates that you need to write a letter of intent that you and your Contractor can read, understand and use.

By the end of this Part, you should be convinced that you need to grab a piece of blank paper and spend time writing a simple letter of intent (using Parts B and C).

4

WHAT IS A CONTRACT?

A contract is a legally binding agreement; a promise that can be relied on and enforced. It doesn't need any specific form, words or style. It doesn't even need to be written down.

> *Where a letter of intent authorises work, [goods and materials] or services to be provided pending the conclusion of some further agreement it will, if accepted, constitute a contract.*[5]

Not all letters of intent *are* contracts. To be legally binding, your letter of intent has to satisfy these five legal requirements:

1 A clear **offer** to pay for specific works

2 **Acceptance** of that offer, either by signed returned letter or by doing something

3 **Consideration** means an exchange of works, goods or services for something of value

4 An **intention** to create a legally binding contract *now*

5 **Certain** and essential terms.

Once an offer has been accepted, then you have created an 'agreement'. Not all agreements are promises that the courts will enforce – all the above five legal requirements are *essential* for your letter of intent to be a contract. In practice they are surprisingly easy to meet:

- Your letter of intent is an *offer* to pay for specific works if the Contractor carries them out.

- Your letter of intent can be *accepted* by email, telephone call, signing your letter or when the Contractor starts to carry out those works.

- Your letter of intent presents *something of value* (often money) *in return* for those works. What lawyers call *consideration* – the price or a promise to do something – is anything of value and can be as inconsequential as a peppercorn or a used sweet wrapper.

- Your letter of intent is sent by one business to another business. *The intention to create a contract* is presumed to exist when there is a business-to-business agreement.

The last requirement – *certainty* – is the one that most letter writers find difficult to meet. This is where you need to focus your attention (Part B).

Why Do You Need Certain Terms? Any contract – even temporary letters of intent – should set out what the parties have agreed with certainty.

Your letter of intent should provide certainty for the *parties*. As the Client, you want to know how much you will have to pay for the initial works, and the Contractor wants to know which works it is carrying out. Certainty ensures both parties know precisely what they have to do. Your letter should also clarify when the initial works are complete – ensuring the Contractor knows when to stop and you know when to oust the Contractor from your site.

Your letter of intent should also provide certainty for *outsiders*, so that an independent third party (e.g. a judge) can immediately understand everything that both parties have agreed to do. If your letter of intent only makes sense because of information you personally have inside your head, then a court may not be able to interpret it or enforce it.

Letters of intent need certain, not vague, terms to create a legally binding agreement.

5

SIMPLE LETTERS START YOUR PROJECT QUICKER

The fundamental purpose of a letter of intent is to help you do business by getting your project underway quickly. There is a right way to start your project quickly and a wrong way.

Let's assume you use an existing letter of intent. Once it receives your letter, the Contractor will need to decide what it is going to do with it. The Contractor can either:

- accept your letter as written and risk missing a legal clause that will come back to bite it, or

- negotiate the terms of your letter and risk missing the deadline to start your project.

The Contractor is caught between a rock and a hard place! If the Contractor is in any doubt, it may start work but it won't sign your letter.

A simple 500-word letter of intent creates trust between you and your Contractor. Even a Contractor working under severe time pressure has enough time to read and understand the 500 words that comprise the agreement. It can decide in minutes whether your letter records the key elements accurately. It knows your letter is not concealing any onerous terms or legal nasties. Trust means your project is more likely to be a success.

After the Contractor has read and understood your 500-word letter of intent, it will have the confidence to either:

- accept your letter as written – knowing that it hasn't missed a legal nasty, or

- quickly negotiate some of the terms of that short letter, but still meet the project start date.

This story illustrates the wrong way to start your project quickly:

Agreement Must Precede Works

In 2003, a £1.68m project for a production facility for packaged yogurts was started under a letter of intent. The letter of intent allowed the project to start quickly. The client sent a second letter when it realised the full contract was still not agreed. Both the client and the contractor let the project continue after the second letter had expired. Neither wanted to stop work to agree the full contract and the client did not want to get a new contractor involved.

The whole project was completed 6 months after the first letter of intent, with the parties still not agreed on the terms of the full contract. The contractor insisted the full contract should be based on a standard form of contract that limited its liability.

It took 7 years and 9 judges to decide whether there was a contract and on what terms. The Supreme Court was unimpressed by the conduct of the parties and said, *The different decisions in the courts below and the arguments in this court demonstrate the perils of beginning work without agreeing to a precise basis on which it is to be done.* ***The moral of the story is to agree first and to start work later.***[6]

You can start your project the right way by writing a legally binding, temporary and effective letter of intent (Parts B and C) that you use properly (Part D).

6

SIMPLE LETTERS RECORD YOUR AGREEMENT PRECISELY

Like any contract, your letter of intent should accurately, briefly and concisely describe what the parties have agreed.

Essentially, using a letter of intent means the parties have not agreed all the commercial aspects for the project, or all the legal terms for the full contract. The parties have agreed that, pending the signing of the full contract, the Contractor can start the project by providing limited works, goods and services (what this book calls 'the initial works').

Your letter of intent does not record the agreement to carry out the whole project. It should accurately record that it is a temporary contract with limited works, that does not extend beyond a few crucial early weeks. Your letter of intent still needs to guide the parties on what they need to do, so it must work as a mini-contract.

You need to check that your letter of intent:

- **Sets out limited works:** You should avoid meaningless and vague phrases like 'preparatory works' or a sweep-up statement like 'all works necessary to meet the project timetable'. The initial works should be self-contained and relatively easy to stop and start; for example if you need to use a different contractor. Accuracy is essential to record that this is an interim agreement for initial works only.

> **TIP:** Check that you and your contract administrator can tell when the initial works are complete (Chapter 11).

■ **Limits changes to those initial works:** Under English law, a letter of intent and the works under that letter cannot be varied except by a new contract. As this is impractical on a construction project, it is better to control the extent of any changes to the initial works. You need a different change procedure in your letter of intent to the one in the full contract.

> **TIP:** Check that your letter permits only limited variations (Chapter 17). Check also that your contract administrator has read your letter of intent so she can use its change procedure correctly.

■ **Continues until the initial works are complete (even if they are delayed):** Your letter of intent should not expire automatically on a pre-determined date, as that might be too soon. Your letter of intent should continue until either the initial works are complete or until the full contract is signed – neither of which can be predicted in advance. The terms of your letter of intent should apply until the end of those works.

> **TIP:** Check your letter does not include an expiry date (Chapter 20).

■ **Contains a get-out (termination) clause:** Your letter of intent will end when the full contract is signed or the initial works are completed. In the meantime, if you discover that the Contractor is incompetent or incompatible, or that your project cannot continue, it is better to end the relationship there and then. Your agreement is not that you will stay together without the full contract for the sake of the project!

> **TIP:** Check that your letter includes a right to terminate the letter of intent (Chapter 18).

7

SIMPLE LETTERS
AVOID DISPUTES

The annual ARCADIS Global Disputes Surveys consistently link construction disputes with failures to:

- Administer the contract (i.e. run the project)

- Understand/comply with the contract's obligations

- Use the procedures in the contract.

If you create a letter of intent that is easy to read, easy to understand and easy to use then you will avoid these key causes of disputes.

Easy to Read: Your letter of intent will be easy to read if it has clear headings, short sentences and simple words. It is a myth that contracts need complex language and jargon.

A 500-word letter of intent helps you avoid disputes because:

- *Your Contractor will read it*: the short length of your letter will encourage the Contractor to read it from start to finish.

- *Your Contractor can negotiate it*: an easy to read letter of intent acts as a checklist for negotiation.

- *Your Contractor can check it records what you agreed*: simple words mean the Contractor can immediately verify whether the letter is an accurate reflection of your agreement.

If your letter of intent is difficult to read, your Contractor definitely won't understand it.

Easy to Understand: Your letter of intent will be easy to understand if it avoids the random content and ambiguity prevalent in existing examples (see Chapter 8). It is a myth that only lawyers should be able to understand the impact of your letter.

A 500-word letter of intent helps you avoid disputes because:

▥ *Your Contractor will have the confidence to raise queries*: with clear and crisp content, your Contractor knows what each word and each paragraph means, and will not be afraid to check if something does not make sense.

▥ *Your Contractor will take responsibility*: when your letter of intent is easy to understand, then the parties can resolve legal and practical issues quickly, without the need to get lawyers involved.

If your letter of intent is hard to understand, your Contractor definitely won't use it.

Easy to Use: Your letter of intent will be easy to use if it accurately covers all that it needs and is designed with the parties in mind. It is a myth that contracts should cover everything the parties can possibly think of, resulting in tedious length. Once your letter of intent contains the four critical contents to create certainty, it is long enough.

A 500-word letter of intent helps you avoid disputes because:

▥ *Your letter of intent builds trust*: when the parties can both use your letter of intent they are more likely to find ways to make it really work, in the process becoming more collaborative.

▥ *Your Contractor wants to comply*: a clear letter of intent leaves no scope for debate about what the Contractor is meant to do – there is no 'wriggle room' and less chance that it will fall back on existing (bad) habits.

These changes can minimise the disputes due to the content of your letter of intent, as well as build better contract relationships.

8

WHAT'S WRONG WITH LETTERS OF INTENT?

Existing letters of intent are full of pitfalls for the unwary and this chapter looks at how you can side-step those pitfalls when you write your letter of intent.

As an example, the City of London Law Society Standard Form of Letter of Intent[7] combines: a contract for the initial works, a section recording the current negotiations on the full contract, financial limits on your liability (intended to encourage conclusion of the full contract), and a fall-back position to say what you will pay if the full contract is never signed. Your letter of intent doesn't actually need all of this!

What else is wrong and how can you avoid these errors?

▨ **Ambiguity:** A recent review of letters of intent highlighted that *ambiguity embedded within [letters of intent] is a fundamental flaw that leads to disputes … the essential terms which the parties should contract on have all been analysed and found to be too ambiguous or poorly drafted to properly perform the role of a legal agreement.*[8]

TIP: Use Part A to ensure you meet the five legal requirements, Part B to write the four critical contents and Part C to write the six effective extras and you will create an accurate and unambiguous legal agreement.

■ **Hedging Your Bets:** Once your letter of intent is sent, there are only two options: you get the full contract signed or you don't. Your letter of intent should not be linked to the full contract. If it gets signed, the full contract applies retrospectively to all the works on your project. If not, your letter of intent needs to work without it.

> **TIP:** Treat your letter of intent as a stand-alone contract (Chapter 6).

■ **Marker in the Sand:** The purpose of a letter of intent is to create a contract for the *initial works*, not to fix the terms for the *whole project*. Your letter of intent does not need to record those terms, which should be in a head of terms document (Chapter 2).

> **TIP:** If you want to include these aspects in your letter of intent because you don't trust the Contractor, think carefully about whether you should be doing any sort of business with that company.

■ **Adopting Full Contract Procedures:** Your letter of intent is meant to be superseded by a comprehensive contract for the whole project. Your letter of intent should nonetheless be self-sufficient.

> **TIP:** Use Parts B and C to ensure your letter contains everything you need in the short-term.

■ **Incentives and Limits:** Your letter of intent is just the first step in the contract negotiation process. There is no guarantee that the Contractor will agree and sign the full contract. No terms within your letter of intent will persuade, cajole or force it to do so.

> **TIP:** Rely on termination to end the Contractor's involvement in your project.

Your letter of intent should record the basics required to instruct the Contractor to carry out *initial works*, and do so accurately, briefly and clearly.

PART

B

HOW YOU CAN WRITE
CERTAIN LETTERS OF INTENT

As a bare minimum:

to have a building contract you ... need agreement as to parties, [works], price and time.[9]

These are the four items your letters of intent *must* contain if it is to be a contract. Without parties and works, there is never a contract. Without price and time, then you may have a contract but it won't provide certainty for the parties.

If your letter of intent is not a contract, then it is no better than a handshake! Before you start, you need a simple process to help you avoid recycling old letters of intent. This process is set out in Chapter 9.

These are the four critical contents:

- **WHO? THE PARTIES:** your letter should explain who is paying for the works (you, as the Client) and who is carrying them out (the Contractor). See Chapter 10.

- **WHAT? THE WORKS:** your letter should specify precisely the initial works *required* to kick-start the project. See Chapter 11.

- **HOW MUCH? PRICE:** your letter should explain how much the Contractor will be paid for carrying out the initial works. See Chapter 12.

- **WHEN? TIME:** your letter should include a date when the initial works will start and a date when they should be completed. See Chapter 13.

Part B will show that an often overlooked but indispensable requirement for your letter of intent is to be *certain about the initial works that the Contractor can get on with, and get paid for, before the full contract is signed.* Without a simple description of the works, you cannot record a fair price or appropriate start and end times.

This Part will help you understand what to write in your letter of intent and why you should keep it simple. Each chapter looks at some of the risks of not writing each element simply and what happens if your letter of intent includes nothing on that topic.

You can easily write the critical content that you need to create a legally binding agreement, dramatically improving the clarity of your letters of intent.

9

BEFORE YOU START WRITING YOUR LETTER OF INTENT

There are a number of stages to writing any document, and these apply to contracts from 1 page (like a 500-word letter of intent) to 100 pages long.

- **Who?** Your letter of intent will be read by the parties, their advisers, any consultant administering its terms and possibly by an adjudicator or court. You should write it to be read, understood and used by all those people.

- **Why?** All writing should have a purpose, especially letters of intent. Consider which of the purposes of a letter of intent (see below) you want to achieve. Keep this in mind.

- **Research:** Part B sets out the four critical contents you need and Part C the six effective extras, as well as what you should avoid. You should only start writing when you know what is needed.

- **Index:** Despite urban myths to the contrary, there is no fixed formula or structure for a letter of intent (or any contract). It makes logical sense to start with the four critical contents (Part B) to ensure that those items are read by the Contractor. But you could write your letter chronologically, party by party, or in any other way that makes sense to you.

- **Text:** The act of writing your letter of intent is a matter of preference – typed, dictated or hand-written all have the same end result. The key is to start from a blank piece of paper and use this book to write down just what you think your letter of intent really needs, and then stop. *Do not recycle* an existing document!

- **Edit it:** Read it aloud. Check that it contains the four critical contents. The purpose of editing is to make sure your letter of intent is accurate, brief and clear.

If you are aiming for perfection, then you will need to *review* it. You can use the 10-Point Scorecard in Chapter 22 to make sure you have covered everything from Parts B and C.

What Is Your Purpose?

The real problem for any writer of letters of intent is to know *why* they are writing and using a letter of intent. You may not need a letter of intent at all. Is the purpose of your letter to …

- *award the contract for the works* to the Contractor? If so, use a letter of acceptance (Chapter 2).

- *settle the negotiations* on the terms of that contract, or *recording the provisions* for the standard form? If so, use a 'heads of terms' document.

- *incentivise the Contractor to sign the full contract?* It won't …

- say *what will happen* if the full contract is not signed? It shouldn't …

- *clarify* the works to be carried out pending signing the full contract on the dotted line? This is the true purpose of a letter of intent.

A letter of intent is the right strategy when you have this last purpose in mind, and when *there are good reasons to start work [before] the finalisation of all the contract documents*[10] (Part D).

10

THE PARTIES INVOLVED

Recording the identity of the parties accurately in your letter of intent is the easiest part of writing your letter of intent. It really doesn't matter who they are. In English law you are free to contract with just about *anyone*.[11]

Whichever company you name as 'the Contractor' on your letter of intent that will be the company you are contracting with. It is almost impossible to persuade the court that you made a mistake which would allow you to escape liability under that letter of intent. In addition to the legal aspect, the identity of your Contractor is also a matter of practicality. As tempting as the white beaches may seem, a Contractor with its registered office in the Turks and Caicos Islands is hard to contact and harder to sue.

Avoiding Common Errors

To ensure your letter of intent names the parties correctly, you should:

- Ask the Contractor for its correct company name, especially when it is part of a large group of similarly-named companies.

- Insert the company number and registered office for a limited company, the trading address for partnerships, and any separate address for notices (including emails, if relevant).

- Check which person is authorised to sign the letter of intent. In practice if the wrong person signs and you entered into the letter of intent in good faith, the courts will allow you to enforce it as a contract.

- Using these details, print a hard copy of your letter of intent on your company's letterhead.

- As Client, email a copy of your letter of intent directly to the Contractor – not through an agent or consultant.

Generally, errors relating to the identity of the parties can be solved by the courts. Most letters of intent follow a tender process, during which the identity of the parties will have become known.

Does It Really Matter?

Keeping an Eye on the Details

Like a letter of intent, contracts made by email are often imprecise, brief and created in a hurry. Following detailed negotiations, an email was sent by a buyer listing the terms that they had agreed with their seller for a transaction for crude oil.

In that email, the buyer accidentally named the wrong limited company as the seller. This was an easy mistake to make as it was similarly named and in the same group of companies. The difference was just a few letters. The buyer's email was agreed by the seller's email titled *Good news*.

Later, the seller wanted to avoid this contract. The seller argued that the contract was not certain because of its incorrect company name. The judge disagreed and would not allow the seller to wriggle out of its contract – it drew on other evidence to prove which company was the intended party. The judge said … *the parties are 'masters of their contractual fate' if they are capable of being identified, even if the identity is not clearly spelt out.* The claim was for an eye-watering $US2.5m plus interest.[12]

Do You Need to Include the Parties? Yes. If your letter of intent does not correctly identify the parties responsible for carrying out its obligations, then your letter lacks certainty and it is not a contract. Getting the parties right is *critical*.

Why Should You Keep It Simple? There are four reasons you should keep it simple. Firstly, it is incredibly quick to clarify the correct details for the parties; secondly, getting it right means you know precisely which corporate entity you are contracting with; thirdly, the consequences of getting it wrong are significant.

The fourth reason to be clear about the parties to the letter of intent is technical (in the legal sense). In English law, a principle called 'privity of contract' means only those parties listed on the letter of intent can bring claims against each other.[13] As the Client, you cannot be sued by a subcontractor if your Contractor fails to pay them – even if the subcontractor knew it was your money funding their works. Similarly, you cannot sue a subcontractor for defective works or a subconsultant for bad design. Your rights are only against the Contractor under the letter of intent. Knowing with whom you are entering into a letter of intent is relatively simple, legally critical and practically essential.

How You Can Write It Simply: Your letter of intent should correctly record three things:

1 the parties

2 their addresses for notices

3 one of:

- the company name, registered number and registered office *for corporations (including limited liability partnerships or LLPs)*

- the partnership name, the names of all current partners and the principal office *for partnerships*

- the trading name, the owner and the principal office *for a sole trader.*

As your letter of intent is designed as a letter, then the 'Client information' is generally found on your letterhead for hard copies and in your email signature for electronic copies. You should add the Contractor information in the heading to the letter or email, and addresses for notices for both parties can be added into the letter as a separate paragraph.

As well as naming the parties, your letter of intent should be signed on behalf of each party by a properly authorised person. In England/Wales that means:

- a director or company secretary *for corporations (including LLPs)*

- all or a specific number of partners (as set out in their partnership agreement) *for partnerships*

- the owner *for a sole trader.*

Partners, directors and company representatives sign as agents for that party and your letter is treated as made by your company or partnership. This method of signing creates a simple contract (see Glossary) and the parties can bring claims for its breach for 6 years from completion of the initial works.

Signing your letter of intent is best practice as it shows the parties have agreed to all the terms in your letter. In fact, your letter can be accepted by email, telephone or by the Contractor starting the initial works.

11

THE WORKS YOUR CONTRACTOR IS DOING

The purpose of your letter of intent is to get the project started without delay. But what does 'starting the project' mean?

As the Contractor is being asked to urgently get on with carrying out works, ordering materials or providing services, it needs to accurately know what those works, goods or services actually are. Is your Contractor:

▨ Carrying out decontamination works?

▨ Preparing the site?

▨ Ordering long-lead materials from far-off lands?

▨ Identifying and analysing risks to finalise a fair price for the project?

▨ Asking its consultants to develop the design to ensure the Contractor's proposals meet your requirements?

▨ Employing site investigation teams to analyse the ground conditions? or

▨ All of the above?

Avoiding Common Errors

To ensure your letter of intent identifies the initial works precisely you should:

- Describe limited initial works so you can tell when they are complete

- Confirm any materials or goods that you want the Contractor to order

- List, if you can, distinct tasks and services that you need the Contractor to perform (ideally just those services that will help you finalise details for the full contract)

- Refer to the works data, specification and drawings to clarify which elements of the whole project are included in the initial works.

Your description of the initial works should ensure that the Contractor knows what it is allowed to do now, and what it can only do once the full contract is signed. Many letters of intent take a vague or 'kitchen sink' approach, which allows the Contractor to start pretty much any works it likes.

A good letter of intent will provide a description of the initial works which is both succinct and sophisticated. The initial works should not be open-ended; they should be clearly defined and limited in scope. The initial works should also be self-contained as it means your letter of intent can, if necessary, be terminated and the project picked up by a replacement contractor.

Does It Really Matter?

It's Not Enough to be Vague

A letter of intent was sent from the client to its contractor for construction work on a property in London covering work described as works already ordered or which may be 'the subject of orders in the future, whether written or oral.' Was this description of the works certain enough to create a contract? The judge reviewed the letter of intent and noted:

There was plainly no agreement as to time ... The agreement as to price was limited to the costs reasonably incurred. There was uncertainty over the identity of the parties ... However, the biggest difficulty comes with a consideration of the [initial works] ... It is based on subsequent orders, instructions and the like which may, or may not, have been reduced to writing.

The conclusion was that if the letter of intent *does not even begin to define* the initial works it is impossible to say that all the terms necessary for a contract are agreed as it lacks certainty.[14]

Do You Need To Include the Works? Yes. As the story above shows, if your letter of intent does not identify the initial works, your letter is too uncertain to be a contract.

That's not quite the end of the story though. Once the Contractor carries out works, orders materials or provides services from which you benefit, then you *will* to have to pay for them. A principle known as 'unjust enrichment' prevents you taking the benefit of works (attached to your land and now owned by you) for free. The Contractor can claim payment of 'a reasonable sum' (known as quantum meruit[15]). However, as there is no contract, you have no rights against the Contractor if it fails to meet your expectations on the extent of the works, the price for those works, and the time to complete those works, never mind the quality of the works. This is a disaster for you and a potential windfall for the Contractor.

Why Should You Keep It Simple? Your letter of intent should be an agreement between two parties to pay for specific works, at a defined price, to be completed by a particular date. Without a limited scope of works, how can you possibly:

- decide a fair price to be paid?

- evaluate if the Contractor is working efficiently and diligently?

- determine what is/not a change to the initial works?

- pin-point when the initial works are complete (and the letter of intent should end)?

How You Can Write It Simply: On most projects, the Contractor is providing a combination of works, information, documents, goods, materials, plant and equipment, as well as services such as supervision, design or payment. A recent review of letters of intent recommends you avoid ambiguity by ensuring that the initial works:

... are relatively simple in nature ... [and] easily distinguishable from other activities; i.e. they can be readily separated from other construction tasks without implying other work not listed in the scope has to be undertaken and can be brought to a stop with a logical cut-off and restart position ...[16]

Your letter should say 'The Contractor will carry out the initial works <insert>' and describe those works accurately, briefly and clearly.

Your letter of intent will be accurate if the description of the initial works makes sense to the parties and other people. It needs to have enough detail and information to allow an independent person to decide whether the Contractor has done what you asked it to do. You need to make sure the reference number, version, date, author and all identifying details of any relevant documents are recorded as these may be superseded during the on-going contract negotiations.

Your letter of intent will be brief and clear if it contains all the necessary information without ambiguities or inconsistencies. While it may be tempting to leave contract details to someone technical, this can result in the descriptions in the letter of intent not matching the details in the works documents (e.g. documents, data, drawings, contract particulars).

12

THE PRICE YOU WILL PAY

The problem with talking money is that everyone *thinks* they are hard done to.

The problem with *not* talking money is that everyone *will definitely* be hard done to!

Many construction disputes, especially adjudications, revolve around whether the Contractor has been paid what it believes is a 'fair' or reasonable price for the works, goods and services provided. Cash is king, or as Lord Denning said, *the very lifeblood of the enterprise.*[17] Knowing how much is to be paid and when is crucial to both parties.

Most[18] UK construction projects are carried out for a fixed price (whether traditional or design/build). This means that the Contractor offers a price to carry out a specific scope of works and, once that estimate is agreed, the Client agrees to pay that price, irrespective of what it actually costs to carry out those works. The Contractor bears the risk that its price is too low and the Client bears the risk that it is too high.

Logically, the initial works should be paid on the same basis as the full contract, because the initial works will be subsumed into the full contract. Generally, your letter of intent should be based on a fixed price for the initial works. Price is a core aim (Chapter 19) of any project.

Avoiding Common Errors

Your letter of intent should:

- adopt the same payment basis as the full contract – whether that is fixed price, remeasurement or other options (see Glossary)

- include a price or rates for the initial works – your letter should not refer to you paying 'reasonable costs' if the full contract is not signed

- meet the minimum requirements for payment set out in the Construction Acts – rather than rely on implied terms under the Scheme for Construction Contracts

- use the price as a limit on your financial exposure (Chapter 20).

If your letter of intent lacks clarity on *works, price and time*, you are effectively signing up to open-ended liability to pay for an open-ended set of works to be completed by an open-ended date.

Does It Really Matter?

The Completed 'State of the Art' Coach Station and Incomplete Paperwork

Mr Clarke asked ACT Construction to construct 'the job' for no more than £815,000. Negotiations proceeded rather informally, relying on honour rather than legal terms. The correspondence (such as there was) revealed that neither the works nor the price were *defined with any precision*. The question was whether there was a contract that met the four critical contents for certainty.

The Decision

The Court of Appeal said, *Even if there is no 'formal' contract, there may still be an agreement to carry out work … even if a price has not been agreed. Provided there is an instruction to do work and an acceptance of that instruction, there is a contract and the law will imply into it an obligation to pay a reasonable sum for that work.*[19]

Mr Clarke had to go to court to discover how much his job had cost: a cool £1.5m.

Do You Need To Include A Price? There are two aspects to consider – *what* you intend to pay for the initial works and *how* you intend to pay for those works.

If your letter of intent does not contain a price, or a means of determining a price, it may be too uncertain for a contract. However, once the Contractor has started on your project, legislation implies a right for the Contractor to be paid a reasonable charge for its works, goods and services.[20]

If your letter of intent does not include a mechanism for paying that price, then the Scheme for Construction Contracts will apply (Chapter 17).

Why Should You Keep It Simple? Faced with an un-priced letter of intent, you cannot tell whether you will pay a fair price for the works involved, and the Contractor cannot tell whether it is going to receive a fair price. If you want to work together, it is critical that your letter of intent provides a fair reward for the works being provided.

An un-priced letter of intent also does not manage the parties' expectations. Is the Contractor hoping for a premium to reflect the rushed nature of these works? Are you expecting normal rates will apply?

Complex payment procedures can lead to you not complying with your payment obligations and having to pay interest and the Contractor being able to suspend work. Late payments may lead to insolvency, as the Contractor will not be able to meet its debts to its subcontractors.

How You Can Write It Simply: The simplest way to write *what* you have to pay is to fix a price for the initial works. Your well-defined initial works (Chapter 11) can simply be priced against the relevant items in the pricing documents; e.g. the contract sum analysis, schedule of rates, or bills of quantities.

You may think that dealing with the *how* of payment procedures is too tricky to simplify. After all, the Construction Acts 1996 and 2009 impose certain minimum requirements on your letter of intent. But as your letter of intent is temporary, you can pay in two instalments and deal with procedural notices simply:

> The Client will pay the price £<insert figures> in two equal instalments and issue pay-less notices. The first payment is due on <insert date> and the final payment on completion of the initial works. The due date is when the Client receives a correct invoice (the payment notice). The final date for payment is 28 days after its receipt. If the Client intends to pay less than the invoiced amount, then it must send the Contractor a written pay-less notice showing how much it will pay and its calculation, to arrive at least 5 days before the final date.

An alternative – simple to write but not to read, understand or use – is to state that 'The payment procedure, due and final dates, and the calculation of instalments is set out in the Scheme for Construction Contracts (amended).'

13

THE TIME TO ACT

It is a sad fact that two-thirds of UK construction projects finish late[21], even once the original completion date has been repeatedly extended. Yet, finishing on time is meant to be the *whole reason* we use letters of intent! Is this the biggest myth relating to letters of intent: that using one will ensure that your project ends on time? There is little evidence to support this tactic.

Given the importance of finishing your project on time, I'm astonished by how few letters of intent actually oblige the Contractor to complete the initial works by a precise date, within a specific period, or to meet an attached programme. How can your letter help your project to finish on time if the works start leisurely? Time is a core aim (Chapter 19) of any project.

Avoiding Common Errors

Your letter of intent needs to encourage the Contractor to minimise delays to the completion of the initial works, and keep your project on schedule. Your letter should:

▨ Include a *start date* for the initial works – this is when the Contractor will be allowed onto the site (and not before)

▨ Require the Contractor to progress the initial works and attend the site regularly

- Specify the *completion date* for the initial works – your letter of intent is intended to hurry the project along, so it must be possible to tell when the Contractor should have finished

- Provide a remedy if the Contractor completes the initial works late – in the form of delay damages (see Glossary).

Your letter of intent is an agreement *used and designed* to speed up the completion of the project and it is therefore vital that you focus on getting the Contractor to keep to time. Your letter of intent should attach an accurate and up-to-date programme, revised to reflect the initial works.

Does It Really Matter?

The Steelwork Debacle

Although the delays and steelwork dispute relating to Wembley Stadium – the home of English national football – are fairly recent, delays due to steel subcontractors are far from new. Back in the late 1970s, a subcontractor was sent a letter of intent asking it to supply and deliver steelwork for the roof of a construction project. To speed up performance of the subcontract works, and hence the main contract, the contractor asked its subcontractor to commence the steelwork pending agreement of the full subcontract.

> ## What Went Wrong
>
> Predictably, the subcontract was never signed as the parties could not agree the prices or delivery dates never mind the appropriate terms and conditions.
>
> The letter of intent failed to mention:
>
> - A start date
>
> - A completion date
>
> - Any rate of progress
>
> - Any remedy if the steelwork was late.
>
> Deliveries were delayed and the main contractor refused to pay for the steelwork as it was late. As the judge said, *Both parties confidently expected a formal contract to [be signed]*. The judge said that the performance of the steelwork was not based on the terms of any contract, including a specific completion date but that the subcontractor was entitled to be paid.[22]

Do You Need To Include Time? You don't have to include a completion date to create a contract. If you don't include a specific date or an agreed programme, the Contractor is under a duty (implied by legislation) to complete the initial works within a 'reasonable time'.

What counts as a reasonable time depends *on the actual circumstances*[23] . The Contractor can be as slow and steady as he likes (not what you want when you are in a hurry). As long as his speed is not unreasonable, you cannot force him to hurry up.

You also don't have to include a specific rate of progress in your letter. But, like a recalcitrant teenager revising for exams, the Contractor can choose to carry out all of the initial works in the last few weeks. There is no implied obligation on the Contractor to attend site regularly.

You also don't have to include a right to deduct delay damages if the Contractor is late in completing the initial works. But, if you don't, you would have to sue the Contractor for breach of the letter of intent, which is more costly and time-consuming than deducting delay damages.

Why Should You Keep It Simple? Having a realistic timetable for starting, progressing and finishing the initial works will provide a standard against which you and any contract administrator can measure the Contractor's performance. More importantly, it helps meet the key objective for using a letter of intent in the first place; i.e. to get the project moving quickly so it can finish on time.

How You Can Write It Simply: Your letter of intent does not need to force the Contractor into a timetable it has no hope of achieving. However, a completion date for the initial works, even if it includes some leeway or contingency, will help the Contractor focus on the project programme.

Your letter of intent can simply say:

> The Contractor will start the initial works on <insert start date>, make regular and reasonable progress, and complete the initial works by <insert completion date>.

Although I have never seen delay damages in a letter of intent, this remedy properly reflects the purpose of using a letter of intent; i.e. to get the project kick-started and to keep it to time. You should seriously consider including a right to deduct (even nominal) damages for each week that the Contractor is late in completing the initial works.

Your letter of intent can simply say:

> If the initial works are not complete by the <insert completion date>, the Client may deduct £<insert figures>, as agreed compensation, for every week that completion of the initial works is delayed.

If your letter of intent includes delay damages, it must also include an extension procedure (Chapter 17). You have to be able to extend the completion date for specific events that delay the Contractor; e.g. if you order changes. The courts will not allow you to delay the Contractor, so it cannot complete the initial works as intended, and also deduct damages for that delay!

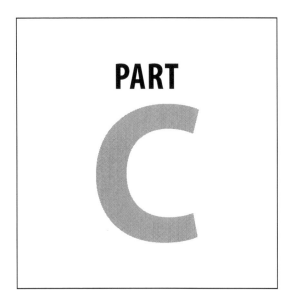

PART

C

HOW YOU CAN WRITE
EFFECTIVE LETTERS
OF INTENT

Once your letter of intent meets the five legal requirements (Part A) and contains the four critical contents (Part B), it will be a legally binding agreement. As a result it creates obligations on both you and the Contractor. If either party does not meet those obligations, it can bring a claim for breach of the letter of intent.

However, to be truly effective your letter of intent requires a little more depth. It should:

- ensure that the works that the Contractor carries out, the materials it supplies and the services it performs have to meet your preferred quality standards (Chapter 14)

- minimise the risks associated with sending a letter of intent and the initial works (Chapter 15)

- prevent those risks undermining your long-term relationship with the Contractor by limiting the Contractor's liability (Chapter 16)

- be 'workable' by including procedures on payment, managing changes to the works and extending the time to complete (Chapter 17)

- set out some useful extra remedies in the event things do not go according to plan (Chapter 18) to help you avoid formal disputes, and

- meet its agreed purpose (Chapter 9), and set out any aims for the initial works and the letter of intent (Chapter 19).

14

THE QUALITY YOU WANT

Many disputes in the construction industry are about the quality of the finished project. Did it meet the parties' explicit and implicit expectations, and objectives? To take just a few examples:

- Should a TV mast have remained standing on Emley Moor, Yorkshire so it could transmit TV signals in snow and hail?

- Should the Torre de Pisa have leant, even before it was completed?

- Should the Millennium Bridge have wobbled when pedestrians crossed the River Thames, London?

- Should the spires on the churches at Chesterfield, England or Verchin, France have twisted?

Achieving the right quality is a core aim (Chapter 19) of any project.

Avoiding Common Errors

Many letters of intent fall into the lazy option of not considering the quality standards required for the initial works. A passing reference to the specification to be used for the full contract may not be enough to cover the quality standards specific to the initial works. Your letter of intent should describe (or refer to documents which describe):

- The functional and aesthetic requirements of the initial works once completed

- The precise specification of goods or materials

- Any tests that the initial works need to pass, and

- The standard for the performance of services including design, workmanship and supervision.

Your letter also needs to distinguish between two measures for quality: an *input* measure (the level of expertise the Contractor should use) and an *output* measure (the extent to which the finished initial works do what was asked of them). This is the difference between reasonable skill and care (input) and fitness for purpose (output).

Unless your letter of intent says so, the Contractor is not guaranteeing that the initial works will achieve your desired result.

Does It Really Matter?

Don't Burn Your Popcorn

Whether your project meets the parties' expectations of its finished quality can make a *huge* difference.

In 2003, ADT agreed to supply a fire suppression system for a Cadbury's new – and not yet built – popcorn factory in Pontefract. ADT used a standard specification to describe what it was providing and what the system was meant to achieve. Essentially, both the client and the contractor focused their efforts on getting the factory operational to provide popcorn to cinemas for the Christmas buying bonanza. Neither of the parties gave a second thought as to the quality the system should meet.

> ### The Dispute
>
> Although the contractor was paid just £9,000, the client claimed £110m for its losses following a catastrophic fire in 2005. Cadbury's argued that ADT failed to provide a fire suppression system that was 'fit for its intended purpose' (a high standard). As the contract said nothing, the Court of Appeal said ADT only had to use reasonable skill and care (mere competence) in designing the system. The crux of the case was that the contract did not specify any particular quality that the client required or the contractor was offering – each thought a different standard had been agreed. The client recovered a paltry £34m.[24]

Do You Need to Include Quality Standards? No. If your letter of intent is silent on the fitness of works, quality of goods and materials, or performance of services, it is still a contract. Terms will be implied by legislation or cases so that:

- works/services will be carried out with reasonable skill and care

- goods/materials will be of satisfactory quality

- goods/materials will be reasonably fit for their intended purpose (provided you have made your purpose known and it is reasonable for you to rely on the Contractor).

These standards are the bare minimum you would expect from your Contractor. Reasonable skill and care simply means that the Contractor is reasonably competent, based on current industry standards, and acts in accordance with generally accepted industry practices.[25] This is a more poetic explanation:

The standard is that of the reasonable average. The law does not require of a professional man that he be a paragon, combining the qualities of polymath and prophet.[26]

Why Should You Keep It Simple? As a Client, you are probably hoping for a little more than Average Contractors Ltd when you appoint your

Contractor. Do you really expect materials which are OK or services provided by a company which is merely competent?

Clarity helps the Contractor to know with certainty what it is being asked to do and to avoid defects – which are largely the result of poorly defined or poorly met quality standards, and the cause of many construction disputes. Keeping it simple at the start pays dividends well into the future.

Despite their length, most letters of intent fail to include any quality standards. Yet, you will have decided to use a specific contractor based on your evaluation of their skills, standards of performance, and experience as set out in their tender. If you have taken the effort to choose an experienced contractor with the right skills and references, then you should not rely on inadequate *implied* terms.

How You Can Write It Simply: If you want the initial works to meet a specific standard or be reasonably fit for their purpose, your letter of intent needs to state what the relevant standard or purpose is. Generally, the tender documents contain specifications, drawings and documents which describe the applicable standards for all works, goods and services.

You should agree the exact standards you want with your Contractor. Your letter must be precise.

Your letter of intent can oblige the Contractor to meet these quality standards by stating, 'The Contractor will use reasonable skill and care to ensure the initial works when completed meet the standards or are fit for the purposes set out in <insert relevant sections of documents>.'

If those documents are not yet agreed, you could give your contract administrator the role of approving the quality of the initial works; e.g. 'the Contractor will complete the initial works to the reasonable satisfaction of Mrs Knight' (assuming Mrs Knight is experienced, knowledgeable and impartial!).

15

THE RISKS YOUR LETTER MUST MANAGE

There is no such thing as a risk-free construction project.

Each site, each end-user, each design and each project team is unique. No-one can guarantee what will happen over the course of the next few months. There might be a global economic meltdown. Steel prices might rise 200% overnight. A flash flood might wash away your site. Your bridge might fall prey to synchronised oscillation, or the bolts on your office block suffer from hydrogen embrittlement. Every construction project involves taking a calculated risk.

Your letter of intent should help the parties manage those risks. There are four stages to risk management – identification, analysis, response and review. Your project should not start until the risks have been properly identified and analysed. If there are too many risks or the analysis shows the project is not commercially viable, you definitely don't want to waste time and money starting on site.

Avoiding Common Errors

Your letter of intent comes into the response and review stages of risk management as it records the parties' response to each of those risks and sets out procedures for reviewing risks as the project progresses. A comprehensive contract would:

- state the specific risks that are allocated to an insurer (e.g. fire, flood, design liability) or one of the parties (e.g. supplier strikes)

- include procedures to review and mitigate the consequences of specific risks (e.g. when you change your mind)

- demonstrate how the consequences of specific risks are shared (e.g. allowing the completion date to be extended for delays caused by a specific risk event, but not allowing the Contractor to claim additional costs).

In practice, many letters of intent absolutely make no provision for risks. As your letter of intent is for limited works, there are two risks that it should address: risks relating to site conditions (the ground risk)[27] and the risk that the full contract is never signed (the contract risk).

Does It Really Matter?
Ignore Risks at Your Peril

Ground Risk: A DIY superstore was being constructed in Stockport on a sloping site. The Contractor assumed that it could use the soil being removed from the high side of the site to back-fill the low side and level the site. The contract said nothing about the quality of the soil. After it had agreed a price for the works, the Contractor discovered that the site was unsuitable for levelling – not only would it have to remove all the soil but it would have to buy in new soil to back-fill the rest of the site. The contractor wrongly believed that the employer bore the ground risk – this mistake cost over £1m.[28]

> **Contract Risk:** On an unrelated case, a Contractor – who started work under a letter of intent – refused to sign the contract. The judge reminded the parties of the *dangers posed by letters of intent which are not followed up promptly by the parties' processing of the formal contract anticipated by them at the letter of intent stage.*[29]

GROUND RISK

Do You Need to Include Ground Risks? No. Your letter will still be certain enough for a contract. If your letter of intent states a fixed price for the initial works, but nothing about ground risks, then the Contractor bears responsibility for the consequences associated with all ground risks. If your letter says nothing about the site, site data and price, you will find yourself liable for inaccurate site surveys and data, and the Contractor may be entitled to more money for unknown and adverse ground conditions.

Why Should You Keep It Simple? There are two key reasons you should proactively deal with ground risk and not ignore it. Firstly, your letter of intent should record the same risk response as the full contract. If your full contract makes the ground risk clear, so should your letter of intent. Secondly, ground risks can be very costly – think Richard III under your car park – and the Contractor may not be able to afford to enter into the full contract if it is surprised by having to pay for unforeseen ground risks relating to the initial works.

How You Can Write It Simply: Your letter can state that:

> The Client will not be responsible for the accuracy of any site information provided to the Contractor; if there are unforeseen site conditions which the Contractor could not discover by visual inspection then the parties will agree reasonable changes to the price and completion date.

If the initial works involve considerable ground risks then it would be far better to use a remeasurement contract (see Glossary) for this part of the project, not a letter of intent.

CONTRACT RISK

Do You Need to Deal with the Contract Risk? No. However, the contract risk falls unevenly on the parties. In the majority of cases, you will have to pay for the initial works under the terms of the letter of intent. You may also have to pay for all other works carried out by the Contractor under:

- an acceptance that your letter's terms apply to all works and the Contractor can rely on an implied term to get paid (Chapter 12) or an express fall-back provision to pay reasonable costs (common in existing letters of intent), or

- a court award for a 'reasonable sum' based on unjust enrichment (Chapter 11).

Why Should You Keep It Simple? The difference for the Contractor is somewhere between its profit margin and loose change. But if the works the Contractor carries out are not under any contract, you can be left out-of-pocket with an abandoned part-completed project to the wrong quality standard that's running behind schedule.

How You Can Write It Simply: You should write a stand-alone temporary agreement for limited initial works (Chapter 6). This agreement should not expire on a specific date (Chapter 20) – it should continue until the initial works are complete, and end naturally when they are complete. You should ensure your contract administrator asks the Contractor to leave the site after completion (Part D).

16

THE LIMITS ON YOUR CONTRACTOR'S LIABILITY

Limits on liability are inextricably linked to risk management. A limit on the Contractor's liability can prevent it being liable for all the costs incurred and delays experienced after a specific risk event has happened.

This, in turn, helps the Contractor provide a more accurate price for carrying out the initial works. The Contractor's price depends on a number of factors:

■ the scope of the initial works (accurately defined, Chapter 11)

■ the risks associated with the initial works (identified and then analysed according to likelihood of occurrence and consequences, Chapter 15)

■ whether the Contractor is accepting total or partial responsibility for those risks, and

■ its analysis of the costs of breaching the letter of intent (realistic requirements, buildable initial works and achievable aims, Chapter 19).

Avoiding Common Errors

Although very few standard form contracts for construction projects limit the *Client's liability*, most letters of intent do exactly that. This is expressed as a maximum amount above which the Client will not have to spend any more money (see Chapter 20 for examples). The most common explanation is that this limit acts as an incentive for the Contractor to sign the full contract, and attempts to control the contract risk (Chapter 15). You should approach such a limit with caution as the argument is unconvincing and, in practice, the limit is rarely effective!

Very few letters of intent limit the *Contractor's liability*, meaning it bears the full cost of all risks, whether or not those risks are identified in your letter of intent. This should increase its price. It also does not reflect the fact that the initial works should be superseded by and subsumed into a full contract which does limit its liability.

Your letter of intent should take the same approach and limit the Contractor's liability. The full contract includes many of these limits on the Contractor's liability: limited damages for delay, limited period to repair defects, a fixed limit on the amount of specific claims, and strict notice periods. If your Contractor would not accept unlimited liability for the project, nor accept limits on your liability under the full contract, why do something different under the letter of intent?

Does It Really Matter?

Unlimited Liability by Stealth

A letter of intent was sent to a steelwork subcontractor, asking it to supply goods. At the time the letter of intent was sent, the parties were still negotiating key issues such as price, delivery dates and the applicable terms and conditions. The subcontractor insisted its conditions were used because they limited its liability. The judge said that when the parties are still negotiating, the court cannot predict what they might finally have agreed and what liability the subcontractor would have accepted. The court said that *It would be an extraordinary result if, by acting on such a request [in the letter of intent] … the [subcontractor] were to assume an unlimited liability for his contractual performance, when he would never assume such liability under any contract which he entered into.*[30]

Do You Need to Include Limits? No. If your letter of intent says nothing, then a limit is implied by way of a strict time period for bringing claims – known as the limitation period. Simple contracts have a limitation period of 6 years after completion of the initial works, whereas deeds have an extended limitation period of 12 years (see Glossary).[31]

There are some limits on the *amount* of any claim arising from breach of the terms of your letter of intent. An innocent party can claim the damages that would put it in the position it would have been in had the letter of intent been properly performed. You cannot recover losses which are not proven, too remote from the breach, or fanciful. The courts can also reduce your damages if there were other contributing factors, or your claim is unreasonable. In an infamous swimming pool case, Mr Forsyth's claim for £35,000 to rebuild his defective swimming pool – it was too shallow – was reduced to a mere £1500 to reflect his disappointment.[32]

Why Should You Keep It Simple? Although all the terms in your letter of intent should be written clearly, there are three factors specific to limits of liability:

1 Limits affect the price. Your Contractor can understand a simple limit on its liability and take it into account in determining a suitable price for the initial works – the higher the limit, the higher the risk to the Contractor, and the higher its price.

2 Limits on liability come under intense scrutiny by the courts. If there is any ambiguity, the courts will interpret them against the party who breached the letter of intent. If you write a limit which is uncertain the courts will throw it out!

3 Limits are controlled by legislation. For B2B transactions, the Unfair Contract Terms Act 1977 only allows a party to limit its liability for breach of the letter of intent if that limit is reasonable. Although this is a complex area of law, a good rule of thumb is that the narrower (and simpler) the term which seeks to limit liability, the more likely it is to be reasonable.

How You Can Write It Simply: Rather than a raft of different limits, for simplicity you could limit the Contractor's liability, for any breach of the letter of intent claim, to a specific sum as follows:

> If this letter of intent is breached, the Contractor's total liability for any one claim, excluding claims arising from death, personal injury or negligence, cannot exceed £<insert figure>.

A limit of between twice and ten times the price is likely to be reasonable and should take into account:

- The price for the initial works

- The consequences for the whole project if the initial works are defective

- The level of any relevant insurances that the Contractor maintains.

The worst that can happen is that your limit is held unreasonable and the Contractor has unlimited liability (the same as if you had no limit).

17

PROCEDURES HELP YOUR PROJECT RUN SMOOTHLY

For most construction projects, the sheer number of people involved and tasks to be completed means that clear procedures are essential to the smooth running of your project. These procedures deal with everything from payment, to communicating information, assisting each other, and managing changes.

Often the day-to-day operation of these procedures is delegated to a contract administrator. Your letter of intent should state which person has authority to 'run' the project and is in charge of ensuring the parties stick to these procedures.

Most letters of intent already rely on industry practices, professional processes and standard behaviours to supplement their express terms. The vast majority of procedures are not written out in full. Some may exist in site manuals or project handbooks, some are 'too obvious' to reduce to writing, and others are unwritten rules of conduct.

Avoiding Common Errors

Your letter of intent should avoid adopting all the procedures from the full contract as this encourages the Contractor to think it *is* the full contract. Likewise those procedures do not necessarily translate well into a temporary contract for limited works. Your letter of intent should include only the processes essential for smooth operation during the initial works.

As your letter of intent covers limited works, it needs just three procedures:

1 **A payment procedure:** required to meet the requirements of the Construction Acts 1996 and 2009 (Chapter 12)

2 **A change procedure:** setting out how/whether the initial works can be extended or varied, including how the parties will agree the impact of that change on the price being paid and the time to complete the works

3 **An extension procedure:** allowing the completion date for the initial works to be extended if the parties agree changes or for other unexpected events. This is important to retain your right to delay damages (Chapter 13).

Does It Really Matter?

Pragmatic and Practical

Change Procedure: A change procedure, or variation clause, helps both the Client and the Contractor. It allows the Client to change the initial works to meet its and the project's changing requirements. It allows the Contractor to carry out the new works without having to re-tender.

The courts have reinforced the sensible use of a variations clause as its purpose is *to enable the [client] to alter the scope of the works to meet its requirements. As a project proceeds it may become clear that some change of mind is needed to attain the result now desired. That might be a simple realisation that something is no longer needed ... or it might be for some other reasons such as lack of money, or a change in the requirements of the actual or prospective occupier or user.*[33]

> **Adopting the Full Contract Procedures:** A court recently decided that even though a letter of intent had instructed the contractor to carry out the initial works in accordance with the terms of the full contract, very few of the procedures were actually incorporated. The dispute resolution (adjudication) procedure did not apply.[34]

PAYMENT PROCEDURE

Do You Need to Include a Payment Procedure? No, but it helps! As your letter of intent is a construction contract, it can either (a) meet the minimum requirements set out in the Construction Acts, or (b) rely on the payment terms implied into it by the Construction Acts.

Why Should You Keep It Simple? Although you can rely on the terms implied by the Construction Acts, those procedures are neither simple to read nor simple to understand. In addition, procedures which are not written down are rarely used properly. It's just not realistic for you to read four pieces of legislation to work out what notices you have to give and when. The Contractor's remedies for your failure to pay are extensive (Chapter 18).

How You Can Write It Simply: See Chapter 12 for a suggested payment procedure for your letter of intent.

CHANGE PROCEDURE

Do You Need to Include a Change Procedure? No. If your letter of intent does not expressly allow changes to the initial works, then you would need to issue a new letter of intent to create a new legally binding agreement for any additional works.

Why Should You Keep It Simple? Whilst changes on your project are inevitable, your letter of intent should not become an open-ended agreement for any and all works on the project. Your letter of intent should be for limited works only.

How You Can Write It Simply: There are two options to ensure your letter of intent does not become an open-ended agreement. Your letter of intent could state that 'Neither party can change the initial works'. This is simple to state but not easy to use.

More practically, your letter of intent could limit the value and extent of any changes, by stating:

> The Client can ask the Contractor to carry out changes to the initial works, provided (a) the parties agree changes to the price and completion date before the Contractor starts the changes, and (b) the agreed changes do not increase the price by more than <insert figure>%.

EXTENSION PROCEDURE

Do You Need to Include an Extension Procedure? You can have a contract without it. But you must have one if you want to be able to deduct delay damages (Chapter 13). The courts will not allow you to prevent the Contractor completing the works by the completion date, *and* retain your right to recover damages for delay that *you* caused.

Why Should You Keep It Simple? A simple extension procedure will allow you to extend the completion date so you both know what date you are aiming for, and retain your right to deduct delay damages.

How You Can Write It Simply: At the minimum, changes to the initial works and delays caused by your conduct should extend the completion date. 'The Client will extend the completion date for any change in the Initial Works or its own acts and omissions which delay completion.' This will be feasible for a temporary period only.

18

REMEDIES HELP YOU AVOID THE COURTS

Although not vital, your letter of intent will be more effective if it includes simple remedies that the parties can use without the need to resort to formal dispute resolution proceedings. Your proposed full contract takes a pragmatic approach and includes a raft of remedies to help you resolve common issues quickly, including:

- Financial compensation for the Client when the initial works are completed late, called delay damages (Chapter 13)

- Grace periods for the Contractor when events outside its control delay completion, called extensions of time (Chapter 17)

- A period during which the Contractor can repair or replace defective parts of the works, called a defects period

- A right to end the contract early, called termination

- Remedies for late payment.

Your letter of intent's key purpose is to get the project started so it can finish on time; but many letters abandon any pretence of encouraging regular works and prompt completion. Speed becomes a toothless ambition rather than a clear contractual obligation. So your letter should include remedies for delay (Chapter 13) and a procedure to extend the completion date (Chapter 17).

Although a defects period is common in contracts for construction projects, it is irrelevant to a letter of intent. If your Contractor is competent and has signed the full contract, defects in the initial works will be dealt with under the procedures in the full contract. If your Contractor is incompetent or has not signed the full contract, you probably do not want them back on site at all, whether or not the initial works are defective.

Avoiding Common Errors

A termination remedy, the importance of which Chapter 6 has already underscored, enhances the temporary nature of your letter of intent. Your letter of intent will be superseded once the full contract is signed, or inevitably end when the initial works are complete.

Most letters of intent do not include a clear remedy allowing either party to bring the agreement to an end when the full contract cannot be signed or when one of the parties commits a serious (and unforgivable) breach of its terms. Instead, they include a right for only the Client to terminate on notice.

This Chapter focuses on ensuring you can end your letter of intent when required.

Does It Really Matter?

Prudence for Pioneers

In a project to build a new type of television mast on an exposed site, the court considered the approach of the parties to this risky project. The project was completed, but within just a few years the mast had collapsed and was no longer transmitting signals.

The House of Lords said, *The project may be alluring. But the risks of injury to those engaged in it, or to others, or to both, may be so manifest and substantial and their elimination may be so difficult to ensure with reasonable certainty that the only proper course is to abandon the project altogether.*

The court said such a course was not unthinkable as *the law requires even pioneers to be prudent.*[35]

Do You Need to Include Remedies? You do not need to include late payment remedies as there are three *implied* remedies that can help:

1 Adjudication: most disputes relating to late or under-payment can be referred to a swift procedure called adjudication

2 Suspension of Works: if you do not pay the sums due to the Contractor in full, and you have not issued a pay-less notice on time, the Contractor can suspend carrying out any or all of the initial works without time or cost penalties

3 Interest: interest is payable at 8% above the current base rate on late payments.[36]

As these remedies are significant, well-known and implied, you do not need to include them in your letter of intent. But please be aware of their potential impact on your project.

On the other hand, you *do* need to include a termination remedy. If your letter of intent does not include a remedy allowing termination, you would need to prove that the Contractor had committed a fundamental breach such as abandoning the initial works. This is a legally complex area of law and one that you can avoid with clear drafting.

Why Should You Keep It Simple? A letter of intent acts like a *probationary period*, and the parties may realise that they cannot work together and there is no point continuing for the rest of the project. If the parties have a simple right to terminate the letter of intent, then you can both walk away from the project, without complicated wrangling or having to bring in lawyers.

How You Can Write It Simply: The termination clauses in your proposed full contract are complex covering a wide range of trigger events, the consequences of termination, sums payable/not payable and so on. Your letter of intent does not need to be as sophisticated as the initial works and period for completion of those works is much more limited. What your letter of intent needs is:

- clarity about when the parties can/not terminate

- a mechanism to notify the other party (written notice)

- a time period between the notice and when the works have to cease (keep it short to reflect the temporary nature of your letter)

- how outstanding payments will be dealt with.

Your remedy should leave neither party tempted to terminate for financial gain, but also neither worried about using the remedy when the circumstances are pointing inexorably to an irretrievable breakdown.

Your letter of intent could say:

If there is a serious breach of this letter, or when it is clear that the parties will not be signing a contract for the project, either party may end this agreement by giving 14 days written notice to the other. At the end of that notice, the Contractor will leave the site in a clean and tidy state and will invoice the Client for a reasonable proportion of the price to cover all initial works started or completed provided that they comply with this letter.

76

19

THE AIMS YOU NEED TO ACHIEVE

There are three types of aims that your letter of intent needs to take account of:

Core Aims: These aims relate to the standard trinity of *time, cost and quality*. Your letter of intent has to strike a balance between getting the initial works started quickly and completed on time, at a price that fairly reflects the other terms of the letter, and carried out to the right quality. These aims are covered in Chapters 12, 13 and 14 respectively.

Co-operative Aim: Although each party has its own *why* for getting involved – its own aim – everyone involved in a construction project instinctively knows that the team has to work together. Any construction project requires the parties to share information, be honest with each other as to the resources they have or need, provide accurate data about progress, and neither hinder nor prevent the others from getting on with their work. Construction is inherently a collaborative process, with myriad tasks occurring simultaneously and sequentially. Back in the Middle Ages, this is how projects were organised, with one master builder in charge of ensuring all the specialist trades worked together to finish the project.

Contractual Aim: Chapter 9 considered some purposes of contracts, including helping the parties do business. One contractual aim is unique to letters of intent. No other contract has this at its heart: the aim being *to keep the project to time by starting the works before all the details required for the full contract have been finalised.*

Avoiding Common Errors

Your letter of intent should not:

- Ignore the core aims of the initial works – even if the quality standards for the initial works are simple to extract from the information for the full project, both the time to complete and the cost for the initial works need to be separately stated.

- Overlook the co-operative nature of construction. Your letter of intent should not treat the Contractor as an adversary, or attempt to ensure you retain the legal and moral high ground. What you need is a simple letter of intent describing how you and your Contractor will work together.

- Disregard its contractual aim. A letter of intent is only necessary when the project needs to start quickly and the full contract cannot be signed. Your letter of intent should reflect these aims by including (1) instructions to start the initial works now and complete them speedily (Chapter 13) and (2) a remedy to allow the parties to end the letter of intent when the full contract is not going to be signed (Chapter 18). Of course, you also need to know how to use it properly (Part D).

Does It Really Matter?

Working Together

Co-operation: The courts reminded the parties involved in a house project of the importance of working together saying, *In the context of a [housebuilding] contract, the emotional commitment of the [client] is invariably high and so the demands on the [parties] are correspondingly increased: the maintenance of good relations between [the team] is therefore crucial.* [37]

CO-OPERATIVE AIM

Do You Need To Include a Co-operative Aim? No. In any construction contract, there is an implied obligation on the parties involved in the project to co-operate with each other. The Contractor cannot carry out any works if you do not provide it with access to the site, drawings and documents, and your instructions when it needs clarification. You cannot manage the project if the Contractor does not tell you what is currently happening on site.

Why Should You Keep It Simple? Although both parties understand in principle the need to co-operate, sometimes in the haste to get the details of the project agreed, and the negotiations on the terms of the full contract, they forget that they are in this together. Collaboration does not come naturally to all clients, contractors and construction specialists. A simple reminder can help the parties focus on the behaviour expected of them.

How You Can Write It Simply: Even clients and contractors with considerable experience in the construction industry, are surprised that they are *obliged* to work together to complete the project. As a result, it is important to use your letter of intent to spell out your understanding of their role and the conduct you expect from your Contractor. You can set your project on the right course by simply stating 'This letter of intent records the Client and the Contractor agreeing to co-operate on the initial works for a project and the provisions that will help define how they carry it out.'

CONTRACTUAL AIM

Do You Need To Include a Contractual Aim? No … but ignoring why you are using a letter of intent is likely to result in misunderstandings. It is not enough to penalise the Contractor when it fails to get the full contract signed. You need to be proactive.

Why Should You Keep It Simple? Getting the project started is the *easy* part of a letter of intent. To be effective your letter of intent needs to include procedures to *keep the project on time* (Chapter 13) and you need to *encourage the parties to sign the full contract.* It is not enough to say that your letter of intent will be superseded by the full contract – that statement is completely ineffectual.

How You Can Write It Simply: The contractual aim of your letter of intent is to ensure its own speedy demise. Many of the contents already discussed help reinforce this aim: your letter needs limited works (Chapter 11), that can only be changed by a controlled amount (Chapter 17). It needs to set a completion date (Chapter 13), with restricted rights to extend that date (Chapter 17) and damages when that date is missed (Chapter 13). As a last resort, if the Contractor can't or won't sign the full contract, either of you can end the letter of intent (Chapter 18). Together these will help keep the Contractor focused on the main prize – a signed full contract entitling it to carry out the whole project.

20

RECYCLED MATERIAL TO AVOID

Part C has focused on six effective extras you need to add to your letter of intent.

Creating your new letter of intent from scratch is the safest way to proceed, especially since the new one will only be 500 words long. However, you may be tempted to recycle parts of previous letters. In doing so, some favoured 'legacy' paragraphs might slip in (unnoticed). These are four remnants you definitely don't want to carry over:

1. Referring to the Contractor's Tender

The tender covers a wide range of meetings, correspondence and pre-contract documents, as well as works, pricing and legal documents. By referring to it, your letter of intent could:

- act as acceptance of the tender, creating a contract for the whole project, or

- accept some of the contract terms referred to in the tender, but without knowing precisely which and therefore creating confusion.

> **TIP:** If you want to make sure you do not create a contract for the whole project, say 'This letter does not accept your tender <insert date> for the Project.'

2. Limiting the Effect of the Letter of Intent to a Specific Date or Amount of Money

What's wrong with these?

Your authority to proceed with the initial works continues until <insert date>, or until payments reach £X, whichever is sooner.

Our maximum liability to you under this letter shall not exceed £X.

The courts rarely[38] limit the amount payable to the Contractor when you have received the benefit of those works (Chapter 11).

> **TIP:** Write your letter of intent with limited initial works for a fixed price and use it properly (Part D).

3. Automatic Expiry on Fixed Date

An expiry date means the legally binding agreement in your letter comes to an abrupt end. You could end up in a contractual no-man's land if:

- your letter of intent expires before the initial works are complete, or

- the Contractor continues carrying out extra works beyond expiry.

Your letter should only end once the initial works are complete or the full contract is signed, not on a date chosen months before.

> **TIP:** Include rights to end your letter of intent on notice and for specific reasons (Chapter 18).

4. Conditions in Your Letter of Intent

If you need to see some items of paperwork before the Contractor starts the initial works, you may be tempted to make your letter 'conditional' on receiving them: *It is a condition of this letter that before you enter the site you must provide us with <insert documents>. If this condition is not satisfied, this letter shall be of no effect.*

Under English law, a *conditional* letter of intent means that any conditions must be satisfied *exactly as set out* before the letter of intent is a binding contract. Why undermine your hard work with this problematic approach?

> **TIP:** If you want to ensure you get that information before the Contractor starts on site, ask for it by email, and wait before sending your letter of intent.

PART
D

NEXT STEPS FOR
LETTER OF INTENT SUCCESS

Now that you've read Parts B and C of this book, you should have a letter of intent which contains the four critical contents and a variety of the six effective extras. It will be simple, robust, workable and significantly better than existing letters of intent. You have also stopped your bad 'recycling' habit, avoiding many of the common errors highlighted so far.

You are now streets ahead of most other senders of letters of intent.

However, this is no time for complacency. Your 500-word letter of intent, by itself, is not enough to create success.

As well as being able to read and understand your letter of intent, you need to be able to use it properly. This means you need to:

▓ ask better questions before you send your new version (Chapter 21)

▓ rate your letter of intent to see if it is 'good to go' (Chapter 22)

▓ after it is sent, focus on getting the full contract signed (Chapter 23)

▓ double-check you have understood all the advice in this book (Chapter 24).

This Part will help you make letters of intent really work for you.

21

BEFORE YOU SEND YOUR LETTER OF INTENT

Although you now have the right content for your letter of intent, you need to ask whether a letter of intent is the right strategy for you, the Contractor and this project. Letters of intent might have worked for you in the past, but the past is not good evidence for what might happen on this project, or on any future projects.

Often, a round-table negotiation to agree the terms of the project contract is as quick and far more effective. Before you send your letter of intent, you need to learn to use letters of intent *wisely*. Ask yourself these questions:

Why Are You Sending a Letter of Intent?

▦ What are the *really good* reasons to start work *now* and not simply wait until the full contract is agreed?

▦ What is the commercial justification for starting now?

▦ Is an early start critical because the project has a drop-dead date beyond which it will no longer be viable; e.g. a project for a specific fixed date event?

▦ Do you or does the Contractor think it will be 'better off' under your letter of intent?

- Have the parties agreed that a letter of intent will benefit the project programme? Have the parties reviewed the current programme to check if provisional times or float can be used instead?

- What bargaining power do you think you will have after your letter of intent is sent? Is the Contractor's contract negotiator going to be involved in the carrying out of the initial works and therefore is unable to get involved in further contract discussions?

- Do you and the Contractor understand the contract risk associated with a letter of intent?

- Do you and the Contractor understand the pitfalls of working without your proposed full contract?

- Are you aware that if your letter of intent does not cover all of the works being carried out, you will still have to pay for those works?

Why Are You Not Signing the Full Contract?

- Have you and the Contractor agreed the commercial terms relating to the rest of your project – parties, works, price and time? Have you and the Contractor agreed the standard form which will be the basis of the full contract?

- If you answered *yes* to both, why not enter into the full contract? If not …

- What makes you, your Contractor or your advisers think that starting the project will make it easier to agree those issues when everyone is busy carrying out works, supplying goods, or providing services?

- Are there clear procedures in place for those key terms to be agreed?

- Is it likely that the outstanding terms will be agreed before the initial works are complete?

Although a letter of intent is meant to be a temporary contract, there are no guarantees that the full contract will be signed. How you, your contract administrator and the Contractor act once the letter of intent is sent will substantially affect its legacy on your project and whether the project is a contractual and commercial success.

22

REVIEWING YOUR LETTER OF INTENT

Before you send your letter of intent, the 10-Point Scorecard (see opposite) provides a last-minute reminder of the ten aspects of letters of intent. Please use it to score your letter and check if it is good to go. For a copy to download or complete on-line go to **www.500words.co.uk/lettersofintent**.

You should also check that you have not added 'subject to contract' to your letter of intent.

That phrase spells disaster as it prevents your letter of intent becoming a contract. It cancels out the presumed intention to create a contract now, which is one of the five legal requirements for a contract. Using that phrase means that *exchange of a formal written contract is [required for] legal liability*[39]; i.e. until the full contract is signed, there is no legally binding agreement.

If you have carefully crafted a letter with the four critical contents, then you should be able to rely on it to create a contract between you and your Contractor. The alternative is a contractual no-man's land.

		-2 marks	-1 mark	+2 marks	
1	**Parties** Is your Contractor willing to work together (co-operate) and ...	A company with a reputation for claims, running late or incompetence?	A new company, or of unknown financial standing and experience?	A reputable company, of good financial standing, known experience and correctly identified?	
2	**Works** Is the description of the initial works ...	Incomplete or generic, and no reference to works documents?	With some detail, but no reference to works documents?	Complete, detailed, with reference to works documents which clarify elements to be provided?	
3	**Price** Is the price for the initial works ...	Not stated or subject to a limit bearing no relation to the initial works?	Reasonable/ proven costs only with no element of profit?	Clearly stated and sufficient for the initial works?	
4	**Time** Are the start and completion dates ...	Unclear, incomplete and unrealistic?	By reference to whole project?	Clear, complete and relating to the initial works only?	
5	**Quality** Are the standards for works, goods, and services ...	Based on fitness for purpose?	By reference to the proposed standard form only?	Based on reasonable skill and care/ or relevant works documents?	

		-2 marks	-1 mark	+2 marks	
6	**Risk** Are the ground risks ...	Not listed, with no reference to survey, and not allocated?	Listed by reference to site surveys, but not priced?	Known and priced?	
7	**Limits** Is the letter of intent limited to ...	A specific sum or date (unrelated to the initial works)?	No specific limit?	A specific sum based on the cost of initial works?	
8	**Procedures** Are the procedures for payment, changes and extensions ...	Included by reference to the full contract?	Unclear or (for payment) rely on the implied statutory procedure?	Clear for payment and change; extension procedure is linked to delay damages?	
9	**Remedies** Is the parties' right to terminate ...	Non-existent?	For the client only on written notice?	For both parties in defined circumstances and on written notice?	
10	**Aims** Does your letter of intent come to an end ...	With a fixed expiry date, not linked to the time to complete the initial works?	With no provision for it to end (contractor gets reasonable costs if it continues to provide works)?	Naturally once initial works are complete, combined with right for parties to terminate?	
				Total Score	

23

USING YOUR LETTER OF INTENT

A letter of intent is meant to be a temporary contract. What happens after the letter of intent is sent depends entirely on you and your Contractor.

Once the letter has been sent:

■ You should *not* get distracted by the works and ignore progressing the contract

■ You should *not* treat the contract negotiation as done and dusted

■ You should *not* extend the scope of the letter by asking the Contractor to do more works

■ You should *not* agree a new letter of intent covering more works

■ You should *not* pay any money over and above the price set out in the letter of intent.

What to Do

Here are some things you and your contract administrator *should* do:

■ Continue to communicate with the Contractor about the progress of the initial works

- Ensure everyone understands the precise extent of the initial works

- Follow the terms of the letter of intent *strictly*

- Ensure payment notices do not exceed the price set out in the letter of intent

- Write to the Contractor as soon as you become aware of the Contractor carrying out works beyond the initial works, to explain that such works are at the Contractor's risk and that, as the Client, you are not required to nor will you pay for them.

> **TIP:** As soon as the letter is sent, schedule a completion meeting – which must be before the initial works are due to finish. Make it clear that you will either agree the full contract, or terminate the Contractor's involvement in your project as allowed by your letter of intent.

If You Never Sign the Full Contract

If the full contract is never signed, then the options range from bad to disastrous!

Option 1: You end the letter of intent and ask the Contractor to leave the site. The Contractor will get paid, depending how you drafted your letter of intent. The amount of payment is often disputed. After termination, you may have to re-tender the project and you will generally face significant delays in getting a new contractor on board.

Option 2: You ignore the contract issues and allow the Contractor to carry on with the works on the site. The only contract setting out the parties' obligations is your letter of intent, which only covers the initial works. You are in a contractual no-man's land.

Under both these scenarios, the Contractor may have carried out extra work not covered by the letter of intent and the price for these works will have to be agreed retrospectively or decided by the courts.

If you cannot agree the full contract, you have to be prepared to walk away. It is better to part ways amicably early in the project, than continue the project on a wing and a prayer. You don't want to end your project with seven years in courts hearing lawyers arguing and judges deciding whether you had a contract and its terms.

24

MAKING SENSE OF IT ALL

Where the 10-Point Scorecard is a robust summary of the *legal* side of things, there are many other guidelines offered in this book which will ensure your letter of intent makes sense.

Work through this Sense-Checklist (see opposite), referring back to the appropriate chapter as needed.

If you can say *Yes* to these questions then you are in the best possible position to use your 500-word letter of intent effectively and create project success.

Like all contracts, letters of intent are tools to help you do business. If you wouldn't use the wrong tool for a specific job at home, then you shouldn't use the wrong letter to do a specific job on your project. As this book has emphasised, the specific job of a letter of intent is to keep the project to time by starting the works before all the details required for the full contract have been finalised. Rather than recycle junk, take the time now to create your perfect tool for that job: a simple, robust and 500-word letter of intent.

Is Your Letter of Intent Certain and a Contract?	Y/N	Chapter
Can you tell who the parties are?		10
Do you understand precisely the scope of the initial works?		11
Can you work out how much the Contractor is being paid for the initial works?		12
Can you identify the start and completion dates for the initial works?		13
Do you and the Contractor understand your respective obligations?		10–13
Is Your Letter of Intent Effective?		
Do you know the performance standard for the initial works?		14
Have the risks related to the initial works been identified and managed?		15
Do you understand who takes the risks involved with the initial works?		15
Does your letter limit the Contractor's liability?		16
Does your letter of intent have the same limitation period as the full contract?		16
Does your letter include payment procedures that comply with the Construction Acts?		17
Does your letter limit the extent of changes to the initial works?		17
Does your letter of intent allow you to deduct delay damages?		17
Does your letter of intent include a right to terminate?		18
Does your letter set out any aims for the initial works?		19
Does the letter of intent make it clear that it does not accept the Contractor's tender?		20
Is the letter of intent unconditional; i.e. does not depend on information, documents or approvals?		20
Will You Prevent Your Letter of Intent Rumbling On?		
Are the parties both ready to commit to the whole project at this stage?		21
Does your letter of intent get a positive score?		22
Are there processes in place to agree the project contract?		23
Are you aware how to act so your conduct does not change, extend or waive any limits in the letter?		23

GLOSSARY

Simple Contract	Also known as a contract 'under hand'. An agreement meeting the five legal requirements (Chapter 4) signed by authorised representatives of the listed parties. Contrast this with a deed. The liability of the parties will last for 6 years from completion of the works.
Deed	A deed is a special form of contract. It must meet the five legal requirements for a contract and it must also (1) state that it is a deed somewhere in the document, (2) be signed as set out by law, and (3) be delivered. The liability of the parties will last for 12 years from completion of the works.
Fixed Price Contract	Also colloquially known as lump sum. A contract where the price for the works is agreed in advance and this is the price that the Client will pay, irrespective of how much it actually costs the Contractor to carry out those works. The price can change if the works are varied or there are other events entitling the Contractor to more money.
Remeasurement Contract	A contract where each element of the works is given a rate; i.e a price per unit. The rates for each element are agreed in advance and the contract sets out estimates of the units for each element. The price paid by the Client depends on how many units are actually provided by the Contractor.
Delay Damages	Also known as liquidated damages (LDs) or liquidated and ascertained damages (LADs). These are a pre-agreed fixed sum per week (or day) payable to the Client for every week (or day) that the initial works are delayed beyond the completion date. They provide a quick and easy remedy for the Client and help keep the Contractor on schedule.
Contract Administrator *	The person named in the letter of intent that (1) acts on behalf of the Client and (2) applies procedures such as making decisions on granting an extension of time to complete the works, agreeing the sums claimed by the Contractor in its invoices, and stating whether the initial works meet the required quality standards. A good contract administrator is essential to ensure your project is a success.
Payment Notice	A notice required under the Construction Acts 1996 and 2009. The notice can be given by either the Client or the Contractor and states the amount the party believes is due under the contract and the basis on which that figure is calculated.
Pay-Less Notice	A notice required under the Construction Acts 1996 and 2009. The notice has to be given by the Client (as the paying party) to the Contractor by a specific date (as set out in the contract). The notice has to state the amount the Client intends to pay and the basis on which that new figure has been calculated. The Pay-Less Notice is required if the Client wants to pay less than the amount on the Payment Notice. If it is not given, or not given on time, the Contractor is entitled to be paid the full amount on the Payment Notice.

FOOTNOTES

1 The Client can be an employer, developer or contractor. This book is written from the perspective of the sender of the letter of intent, as it is normally in control of the content of the letter.

2 His Honour Judge Richard Seymour QC in Tesco Stores Limited v Costain Construction and Others [2003] EWHC 1487 (TCC).

3 The definition is set out in the Construction Acts 1996 and 2009 (the Housing Grants, Construction and Regeneration Act 1996 and the Local Democracy, Economic Development and Construction Act 2009).

4 See the NBS National Construction Contracts and Law Surveys.

5 Durabella Ltd v J Jarvis & Sons Ltd 83 Con LR 145 [2001].

6 RTS Flexible Systems Ltd v Molkerei Alois Müller GmbH & Co KG [2010] UKSC 38, Lord Clarke.

7 Available from the City of London Law Society website.

8 Russell Bailey and Wayne Lord in their unpublished masters dissertation: Letters of Intent: Avoiding the old mistakes, again [2013] Loughborough University.

9 Hart Investments Ltd v Fidler [2006] EWHC 2857 (TCC).

10 See Cunningham v Collett & Farmer (a firm) [2006] EWHC 148 (TCC).

11 More accurately, you can only contract with someone with the capacity to contract, which excludes minors (people under 18 years of age), with mental capacity (so excluding mentally ill people) and with companies acting within their powers.

12 Glencore Energy UK Ltd v Cirrus Oil Services Ltd [2014] EWHC 87.

13 This was changed by the Contracts (Rights of Third Parties) Act 1999 and third parties can sue if the party does or purports to confer a benefit on him or his class of people. In practice many contracts expressly state that no third parties can sue under this Act.

14 Hart Investments Ltd v Fidler [2006] EWHC 2857 (TCC).

15 Known as quantum meruit, literally 'as much as is deserved'. This is payable under an equitable principle referred to as quasi-contract or unjust enrichment.

16 Russell Bailey and Wayne Lord in their unpublished masters dissertation: Letters of Intent: Avoiding the old mistakes, again [2013] Loughborough University.

17 Gilbert-Ash (Northern) Ltd v Modern Engineering (Bristol) Ltd [1973] 3 WLR 421, House of Lords decision.

18 See e.g. NBS National Construction Contracts and Law Survey 2015 where between 50-75% of respondents said the pricing mechanism most often used for their projects was a lump sum or fixed price basis.

19 Clarke & Sons v ACT Construction [2002] EWCA Civ 972.

20 E.g. s15 of the Supply of Goods and Services Act 1982 (as amended).

21 The latest UK Construction KPI figures are available from Glenigan. This data is from 2015.

22 British Steel Corporation v Cleveland Bridge and Engineering Co Ltd [1984] 1 All ER 504.

23 Hick v Raymond & Reid [1893] AC 22. Lord Watson said that a reasonable time "has invariably been held to mean that the party upon whom it is incumbent duly fulfils his obligation, notwithstanding protracted delay, so long as such delay is attributable to causes beyond his control, and he has neither acted negligently nor unreasonably."

24 Trebor Bassett and Cadbury v ADT Fire and Security [2012] EWCA Civ 1158.

25 Bolam v Friern Hospital Management Committee [1957] 2 All ER 118.

26 Bingham LJ, Eckersley v Binnie & Partners [1988] 18 Con LR 1.

27 For new build projects, these are largely below ground conditions. For refurbishment projects, site risks relate to the discovery of asbestos, integrity of existing structures, and so on.

28 Mowlem Plc v Phi Group Ltd [2004] BLR 421.

29 Diamond Build Limited v Clapham Park Homes Ltd [2008] EWHC 1439 (TCC).

30 British Steel Corporation v Cleveland Bridge and Engineering Co Ltd [1984] 1 All ER 504.

31 Limitation Act 1980 ss5 and 8.

32 Ruxley Electronics and Construction Ltd v Forsyth [1995] UKHL 8.

33 Abbey Developments Ltd v PP Brickwork Ltd [2003] EWHC 1987.

34 Twintec Ltd v Volkerfitzpatrick Ltd [2014] EWHC 10.

35 Independent Broadcasting Authority v EMI and BICC Construction [1995] PNLR 179, HL Lord Edmund-Davies.

36 As required by the Late Payment of Commercial Debts (Interest) Act 1998 (as amended).

37 West & Anor v Ian Finlay & Associates [2013] EWHC 868 (TCC).

38 Mowlem Plc v Stena Line Ports Ltd [2004] EWHC 2206 (TCC) contains a good example of a limited letter of intent, upheld by the courts.

39 Bennett (Electrical) Services Limited v Inviron Limited [2007] EWHC 49 (TCC).

ABOUT THE AUTHOR

Sarah Fox has spent 20 years reading, analysing, critiquing, writing and training others on using construction contracts. At Eversheds LLP, she wrote, adapted, amended, negotiated and resolved disputes on contracts from 1 page to 100 pages.

She now specialises in helping construction professionals to build simple contracts. With JCT SB 2011 weighing in at over 50,000 words plus another 25,000 words of amendments, the simplicity of writing 500-word contracts has become Sarah's personal project.

Simple means short, readable, understandable and usable. 500 words is roughly a single A4-page. Her contracts are elegant, clear and brief, and – most importantly – legally robust.

With this book as your guide, you can create simple letters of intent. To get additional support, readers can sign up for Sarah's emailed newsletter, download a letter of intent template and get exclusive access to on-line versions of the 10-Point Scorecard and Sense-Checklist as well as a host of handy resources for construction specialists.

Sarah is an award-winning keynote speaker and is available to help construction companies who are ready to cut their contracts down to size to make them easier to read, understand and use.

www.500words.co.uk

sarah@500words.co.uk

A THANK YOU CARD

This book only exists because my idea became a reality with the help of fabulous friends, family and supporters. But in the interests of simplicity I want to highlight just a few. My main thanks go to Robert Watson, my editor, who crafted my ideas and words into a coherent whole and even admitted to liking the case law interludes, and who wrote the simplest contract I have ever read.

The idea for a 500-Word contract came during a conversation waiting for a train at Euston station with my twin sister, Emma Sutton. She dedicates herself to helping small businesses find their message and she helped me find mine.

The lecturing team at Salford University, particularly Brodie McAdam and Paul Chynoweth, helped me turn my SCL Hudson Prize paper on Letters of Intent into a peer-reviewed paper in the International Journal for Law in the Built Environment, and set me on the path to writing this book.

Lastly, my husband Brian who provides the encouragement I need to step out of my comfort zone, and away from my desk.

Printed in Great Britain
by Amazon

15198958R00062